THE FALLS

October 2020

POEMS BY

EMILY MOHN-SLATE

For mike,
with gratitude for
your support and your example
as a teacher and big-hearted
person —
Thank you!
Emily

newamericanpress
Milwaukee, Wis.

n e w a m e r i c a n p r e s s

www.NewAmericanPress.com

© 2020 by Emily Mohn-Slate

Printed in the United States of America

ISBN 9781941561232

Book design by Charli Barnes
http://www.charlibarnes.com

For ordering information, please contact:
Ingram Book Group
One Ingram Blvd.
La Vergne, TN 37086
(800) 937-8000
orders@ingrambook.com

For media and event inquiries, please visit:
https://www.newamericanpress.com

For Nico

CONTENTS

THE FALLS

Red is the strangest pain to bear.

—*Charlotte Mew*

I

SO EASY

A woman forgot her baby in the park. People found it
murmuring in the bushes, called it *Fairy*.
I want to keep sleeping when his yell slices twilight —
not feed the baby, whose appetite is unfeeling, total.
The baby grunts, spits — I want to be alone,
but it would be good for me to go out with the baby.
If I keep walking, he keeps sleeping.
A woman at the park's edge holds honey petals
to her nose, breathes them the way I breathe
the baby's furry head. A woman left her baby in the car,
rushed to work — her baby overheated & died.
I forget things so often now. I never forget my glasses.
It would be so easy to forget the baby.
Old bikes lie on porches, washed in yellow light,
exhausted. I hover two fingers above
his chest, search for breath. I love to hear
the baby's slight gasp when I turn on a light —
I study his open mouth, flick the light on
& off & on until I can't. I forgot my keys,
my jacket. A woman drove off with her baby on the roof
of her car. Did I fasten the buckle around
the baby's soft waist? I didn't want to come out today,
but it is good to smell the oily pizza boxes at Pino's,
to dodge the garbage truck lumbering
down Hastings Street, men hanging on by a tiny crescent.
They found her baby at 45th and Cholla
on the highway line, alive, not even crying.
I had a hat once that I loved, red and blue wool.
I lost & found it in a Shaw's parking lot, mashed down,
brown with exhaust. I washed it by hand,
hung it up to dry. The baby licks the stroller harness,
wets the rip-proof vinyl to a deeper red.

ANATOMY OF DISTANCE

There are machines for this—

lifting back the skin of the map
so the border can be laid down again,

the pieces of river
placed at an easy angle.

Be sure you won't slice
any place you can't handle

seeing stripped. Carry a tape measure
set to whip back

when you've gone too deep.
The hills keep humming their low sounds.

A sextant flattens the terrain
but the eye unaided

is sharper than a shark's tail.
Distance is best left in rain,

to soak until the pages
clump, wet mush

of the actual world.
Cut the sweep spare

enough to throw across a bridge,
a sturdy one, so you can cross looking down.

Water makes you want more
distance, and distance starts to resemble

other things—your yellow tie,
the orchid crumpling on your windowsill.

From here, anything
can be another thing.

I labored to open the cardboard box, sheathed as it was
in layers of tape. The dress-preserver had taken more precautions

than necessary, as the undertaker seals the coffin just so, certain
it is inviolable before cradling its heft into earth.

No dirt, air, or touch could sully its pristine whiteness.
Like Waterhouse's *Ophelia*, it lay alone in repose, vacant, the wedding dance

a mere watery dream. I can't remember when the branch cracked
and it slipped into the river.

When I finally exhumed the dress shaped to the contours of my younger body
in love, I fell to my knees and howled.

It never occurred to me on that wedding-belled day how funereal its billowing
seams were, or how I would unearth it, alone,

from a basement darkening an apartment in which he will never live.

DEAR CHARLOTTE MEW

July

Before I heard your voice on the page,
   I was afraid my words were not enough.
But your peculiar music stirred

the loneliest fields in me.
   What is it about her? my friend asks.

Is it enough to say our wounds are sisters?
   When you died, the reporter wrote: *Charlotte New* [sic]
said to be a writer. It stung me, too.

In Hampstead Cemetery, I look
   for you—bend to each misshapen name
hot, confused, so many Charlottes
   who aren't you, trip over sticks and dents

in dry grass. Apologize to the dead, jump
   when birds peal from willows at my head.
Sorry, sorry, I say to your neighbors.
   Swig of water, hunch lower to see—

your marker. Straw grass thickets your sunken
   plot, almost erases the day you died—
Dante's line still clear:
   Cast down the seed of weeping and attend

I lie down in your grass—it pricks my fingers.
　　Such slight inches of earth between us.

Did you write a note before
　　you poured Lysol into the glass?
Did they bury you in your suitcoat?

Everybody thinks that you are dead, / But I.
　　What good to say?
I'm glad I found you.

LIGHTNING FLOWERS

My daughter is finally asleep
in my throbbing arms.
She grows roots that branch
around my skin.
The woman next to me
on the plane, who let my wild
baby grab her rings, lick the zipper
of her purse, waving away
my apologies, sleeps now, too.
On her tray table, her
highlighted hair a perfect
frosted cake.
Lois, married 38 years
to her second husband
who died recently—
He was a good one, she says.
A really good one. It changes everything.

Lois was surprised
I have a second husband too.
My first husband, a heavy bell
still ringing —
my second husband, clear
light on green leaves.
Maybe it was supposed
to be this way.
What do I know?
In her sleep, my daughter
clutches my shirt collar—
the edge of a boat
in her dream.
Through the crack

in the seats, I watch
a movie —no sound—
Tilda Swinton, Ralph Fiennes,
& two younger actors
eat pretty food, give each other
meaningful looks.
Then some betrayal
and they all go crazy.
Tilda glides around in
a white sheath, big aviators.
Her sleeves billow like cool air.
No baby to bounce.

We coast into purple-black
clouds, to a forest of
lightning trees on the horizon.
The last time I saw my first
husband, he was wearing
a wool jacket, oxford shoes,
living alone in a loft.
Just the right amount
of silver laced his beard.
He seemed happy.
I think about my husband
at home—the one who said
you deserve to be loved well.
We fly into light
slashing the night's skin,
burning up the sky,
& she wakes—I start
bouncing again, sing
twinkle twinkle little star
in her tiny ear, lightning
cradling our plane,
how I wonder what you are—

branches barreling down—
the future the most
beautiful, terrible thing.

THE FALLS

Galloping horses,
water twisting over

rock edge, a green-grey pour.
Long-fingered voices

luring. Heavy creatures,
we were not made to rise.

The mist curves a fist,
coiling to strike.

I will hide inside.

A woman on her honeymoon
climbed down to the falls alone.

She picked her way over
scum-slipped rocks and disappeared.

Barely alive in her hospital bed,
she told reporters, *I wanted*

to touch beauty. It was like
a tornado pulled me in.

THE ANT'S SMALL FACE

Let me sing of the ant
who moves across
linoleum, black cast,
hollow-cheeked, weaving
away from the avalanche
of my folded paper towel.
Let me swing open
my cupboard full
of salty things, scrounge
for what I want.
In half-light, it weaves
up the fake Tiffany lamp,
scrambles its high knees.
I know it will take
whatever sweetness
it finds back to others
who will share the loot.
Let me show you how
I bring my hand down
hard, regretting briefly
what has to be done.
But first let me take
its nervous face
in my hands and ask it
to show me how
to keep going
when the hand
of something immense
hangs above.

STILL LIFE WITH EX-HUSBAND LINGERING

The new couple downstairs, circled
by their gleaming grill, deck furniture

and potted herbs arranged just so,
clink their plates after dining alfresco,

then rest together, and talk of the baby.
I trace a pale shadow on my ring finger

with my thumb the way I used to trace
my ring. His half-packed boxes line the walls

of our tiny walk-up. The ring hums
too loudly in my jewelry box.

I'm done with the courage
I've needed for the last year.

The new couple doesn't know
I'm up here stewing through the screen.

Or that once he leaves, I will drive
a butcher knife through the couch cushions.

NEEDLEWORK

"The father had been wise to show them before his death
that work is a treasure."
— Jean de la Fontaine, "Le Laboureur et Ses Enfants"

Next door, men cut off the trees' hands. Their machines hum
as they work. A woman drags a line of children two-by-two
straining under the weight of giggling bodies.

People say, This is how the world works.
At the gym, the manager watches someone else
buff an already spotless floor.

My father told me to do what I loved to do —
one third of my life will be work. Every day, he arrived home
ashen, hiked the basement stairs broken by long pauses.

I lick a sympathy card shut, drop it in a blue box
and the cows are knee-deep eating green.
I give an A, a B- , a C+. This, the sum

of our work, but not why—
the men pile lifeless branches into the truck bed.
I think I hear them singing.

A woman drags a hose to water the leaves along the wall,
leaves no one will see, under a highway behind a hotel gate.
I watch her from my treadmill through a glass wall.

TO THE QUESTION, "WHAT HAPPENED?"

He grabbed
the roll of quarters,

lifted it high —
I just don't think

*I can be married
anymore —*

then cracked the casing
on the table's hard end.

The paper was tight —
wouldn't give at once —

The second swing spilled
coins across the floor.

Smell of dust without rain,
sound of air.

*If you don't think,
then you know,*

I said, stooping to find
each cold coin.

STILL LIFE WITH RESCUE DOG

Years ago, we adopted a hound and named him Sounder.
    In the book, the boy goes looking for Sounder and finds

        only blood and an ear. The mother tells the boy,
                You must learn to lose, child.

        He sleeps with the ear, clotted with dirt, crushed
        under his pillow, waiting for Sounder's return.

*

We were charmed by the dog's wise eyes, high hips,
    how he'd scare the purse-dogs on Walnut Street.

        Even his sob story was perfectly sad:
        owner a drunk, he'd put the dog in a burlap sack with rocks

        to drown him in a pond.
But there was our dog, tap-dancing the wood floors

of our attic apartment, baying through weak walls.
    We had to work, we were young and poor,

        hadn't thought it all out, what the dog would need.
He flung his bulk against the crate's bars until his shoulders grizzled.

*

We couldn't keep him. I cried for weeks,
said it felt like a miscarriage.

    We took Sounder, tail flapping, wet nose poking
    the back of my neck, back across the river in our Volkswagen.

My cart glides into
the frozen foods aisle

and there he is, unloading
bags of frozen peas,

ripping the box open
with his blade.

You look good, he says.
I return the compliment

and wish I didn't mean it.
We laugh about the time

he slipped and fell
trying to moonwalk

on our kitchen floor.
Laughing with him

is harder than anything
now. It punches the bruise

I bury deepest down —
he is not a monster —

his quick humor still useful
as the knife in his palm.

I push my cart away
and after a few seconds

look over my shoulder.
His back is foreign.

A country I once felt
was my own.

THUNDERSTART

We're in the sea when the rain comes hard
My new lover runs to shore   his legs
slick and purposeful

to build a canopy of umbrellas
over our bags
on a cracked plastic chair

When he's done
he stands and watches
to make sure it doesn't fall

I didn't ask him to do this   to build
a thin roof over our things
I'm afraid I'll get used to this kindness

From somewhere up in the leaves
thunder starts
I worry in the water

Knowing he will come to me soon
I float on my back
open my mouth

to warm rain
instead of the wavering architecture
of his promises

DEAR CHARLOTTE

July

> "*The others have gone; they were tired, and half afraid,*
> *But I would rather be standing here.*"
> — "*In Nunhead Cemetery*"

I wish you were famous enough for them
to have kept your home intact. Doty visited Whitman's
stuffed parrot, but who knows where your Wek is decayed.

Today is hot for England, high July—
A family picnics near your plot, laughing.
A child drips an ice cream cone onto a grave.

On the way here, I passed the London Pride parade.
I imagined you holding Ella or May's hand
instead of your own faded lapel.

Charlotte, can you smell the sea?
It's not far off. Out there, you can float for miles,
try out your voices on the wind.

When you come to my door on Elysian Street,
I will ask you in. I will plant you a bougainvillea,
water it until the bright petals blaze.

When you met yourself at your door,
which face did you see, wet with rain?
At your grave, weeds wash your plot with weak colors.

I will stay until the moon finds your grave,
until the rooks arrive
wearing their slick black coats.

DROWNING THE CRACKS

When my nephew went to kindergarten, everyone told him, *You're a big kid now!* First day, a terrible thunderstorm — the lights went out, stayed out. Mrs. Peters played music to drown the cracks. *It didn't work*, he said — *I could still hear it.* He locked himself in his room every morning for two weeks. And here I am now, lying in the pitch-black, a new lover snoring beside me, straining my ears for thunder, the terrible light that means the crack is coming. Everyone telling me, *Don't worry. It will be fine.* The light hits the room and all I have are my own hands, two dead fish.

OPEN TOP BUS TOUR, ISLE OF SKYE

The wind blows spiteful across this high green land—
our hair tangles in impossible knots. My new husband

and I huddle into each other in thin coats,
ask the driver to stop for pictures.

A woman alone on a moor paints her roof red —
There, amid cold orbits of greens and browns,

a red roof. Her hair is silver white, she lets
the bucket hang in the crease of her fingers

as she climbs the ladder. But I do not
take her picture. The sky flecks blue and grey,

more blue than the freezing sea. A basalt castle,
ruins in a field nearby.

The driver says, *the son of a chieftain dropped
from a castle window and died on the wet rocks.*

*The nurse was shoved to sea in a small boat,
the castle left to crumble.* What kind of tourist comes

to this northern land? People who think wind,
rock, and sea mean romance, who think what is hard

and stunning must be ancient and true.
I can't tell him I feel alone even on our honeymoon.

As we pass the woman painting, I crane my neck
and halfway stand to see her carrying another bucket

up the ladder, her figure swallowed by the sea.
Once we're gone, there's no one watching.

The wind rocks the ladder. Look what her red
can do against the scrubbed grey sky.

STILL LIFE WITH POSSIBLE LIFE

I stood in the green-brown
clearing of Frick Park
trees bowing to reach
the skinny creek

The place I'd walked every day
for two years
no body with me
but his leaving never leaving me—

How could he leave—
the only body   sharing my air

But that Tuesday
a door opened in the leaves
crackle of light   a possible life

while that other door
gnarled carvings of bruise upon day
of wound upon years
started easing closed

and the air was my own

and when I asked him to go
I said *Please*

MAYBE

This week's email update:
you may be able to feel the baby's kicks.
Other news: twelve illegal miners
hauled up from an abandoned gold mine
hundreds more decomposing underground —
a 25-year old woman hacked to death
with a meat cleaver in Delhi,
walking to meet her cousin's new baby —
a plane missing over Nepal
over the mountains where we
ate mango on twin beds pushed
together, unsealable crack between
bony mattresses, & talked about babies,
how maybe we were ready.

IN THE NEWARK AIRPORT BATHROOM

teeth rest on the wet counter,
              pale pink gums with white-yellowing bits.
Teeth, in no rush for a mouth or a face.

The woman they were made for
              hunches beside me at the sink
hair loosening from a bun.

Maybe she's sick — I can't tell.
              She cups faucet water into
her mouth, swishes and spits.

Do they fit her gums cleanly?
              I wonder if she will slip them back in
to eat, what her children think,

if it makes them think of her age,
              like my mother's new hip
makes me think of hers.

How each time she steps,
              the part the grease can't reach
creaks. Each step,

she swings, curving like a bell,
              ringing out, *I'm mortal I'm mortal,*
and so are you.

AS MUCH AS A LETTER

I bleed through the night what may be his body, all his little parts forming. I want to talk to him, to ask him to stay, but maybe he's already gone. I'm never one to ask someone to stay if he wants to go. It would be easier without him. For weeks, he's been burrowing in my belly according to some code, no regard for me. I'm shedding clots with thick heads; they trail pink to black in water. Maybe I do want him. He's in my black blood, curled in my bones — all these parts I can't name, he feels. At the hospital, a nurse pushes me down bland hallways in a wheelchair. A robot follows us, a cart of supplies with no pusher. I don't want to bet against him again; he's there. They say he weighs as much as a letter.

DEAR CHARLOTTE

November

My shoulders wedge into a box hammered shut by others, their needs heavy on my chest. I see you in those rooms *where for good or ill — things died.* How much weight were you buried under? Making sacrifices for women who found you clever, amusing, not enough. *I shall never touch your hair, or hear the little tick behind your breast.* In your dim row house, making tea for your mother, unable to leave your gentle sister — how much weight, Charlotte? Could you hear the shovel ramming down? Maybe the trees will understand, *wise trees that do not care.* Dirt sifting in through the slats. I feel clumpy grains on my tongue, spit them out, listen harder for your voice. For decades, you clicked down Theobald's Road, pork pie hat, men's suit, umbrella in hand: *Red is the strangest pain to bear. A rose can stab you across the street deeper than any knife.* Only you could say it that true —The kindest words can be the cruelest, and *my soul is red,* too. What I mean is, you are the only one who might hear me, and you are still dead.

WEDNESDAY MORNING AND I AM BEING OPENED

After peeing in a cup and printing my name,
I think cancer and wait for them to shine light
on my inside walls, to extract their sample.

I tell the nurse I'm nervous. Her voice is stiff —
You'll be fine, the way people who hate kids talk to kids.
My thighs, already hot, press tighter.

The doctor sits down, asks me to inch closer,
splay my legs. She moves below me, cranks me open
with her metal, says, *You're so tense. You're fighting me.*

It's hard not to, I say and think about the boy who sat
behind me in eighth grade homeroom, how he'd lean up
and tell me *Your ass looks nice,*

how my body recoiled, felt out of control
even though I was sitting at my desk,
careful not to bend over.

I lie flat on the table, hands knuckled over
my stomach in prayer, begging my cells
to stay quiet, to sit up straight.

WINDOW

           Sarah's husband is dating someone
and she's in love with someone else
           but they still share a bed.
She can't talk—her kids
           are always around.
I get snippets by text:
           I don't know what happened—
how we fell apart.
           Tonight, my baby quiet
in his crib, my husband
           folded in our bed, another
baby kicking inside me—
           I stand for a long time
in front of the stained glass
           window in the hall.
Someone soldered these
           planets of glass together
formed a pattern
           and lined it with lead.
Marigold, rose, blue—
           the window has warped
with age, is missing teeth.
           Dull streetlights
cast waves in the glass
           that sunlight
blots out. I run my hands
           over the rough landscape
of colors— bright leaves
           by day, now night shades
between
           these sleeping bodies
I love. How finite

        my people are.
I feel the weight
        of their breathing—
of this life we've built.
        How it chokes and
burrows, how even dreams
        change us, scraping
glacial paths inside.

WOMAN AS COLUMN, FITZWILLIAM MUSEUM

"Will Nigeria's abducted schoolgirls ever be found?"
— BBC News, May 12, 2014

What made her particular is lost. She towers
above the room with sunken stone hair,

the temple roof vanished from her head.
Buried in a dung heap up to her neck,

her people planted her deep to help grow
their crops. Before the professor wrenched

her out, he bribed the Turks in charge,
traded a telescope for her generous body.

Off a cobbled Cambridge street, priestess
of Demeter's cult, stock-still, bleak lips shut,

she watches us among mouthless strangers
and water pitchers, a Gorgon head

between her breasts her only working eyes.
Just having a body can be deadly.

ELLIPTICAL ADVICE

after Harryette Mullen

Sleep now because soon…what no one tells you is…I loved being…

you cannot imagine the…you have to…you never know…I thought

it would be…of course, you just do whatever…on the other hand, she

says it's better…don't believe them when they…the baby will

make you…sometimes, you will want to…you're always gonna

need…you won't be able to…it's crazy, but…before the baby comes…

LANDSCAPE WITH DREAM, DEER

The man who left me
returns as a deer

black eyes
rich as dirt

insisting on
forgiveness

his belly speckled
and wild

I am not able

KINDREDS

How I have survived

my friend saying *I know you will get through this*

                    I don't know how, but you will

*

the way her kindness is surprise sun

*

She knows the veil between life and death

is just a curtain of noisy beads

she keeps me

on this side

her face blotching red
so I tried the elephant the giraffe
the caterpillar her finger my finger
    I opened the car window
      & gripped her sweaty hand
      & after the seventh song I tried
ABCDEFGHIJKLMNOPQRSTUVWXY&Z
Now I know my ABCS Next time won't you sing with me?
she stopped crying & stared at me & stayed that way
so I kept singing for 40 minutes
      I was afraid to stop
      her eyes on my eyes   singing & looking
      rocks grinding my throat   jaw coming loose
      I sang & sang & sang   until
          her eyes shut   her hand loosened
             as if she was falling
                into the arms of a kind water
                  where I couldn't find her
                but she would be safe
                  & the red left her

how was your day? someone asked

& last night I bounced on the edge of a hotel bed
holding her in my arm's crook
& under my breath I whispered
    What the fuck What the fuck
    please sleep please sleep please sleep
    why why why why why why why
& my friend was pouring a bourbon for herself in her kitchen
& the face in the window across the street turned off the light
& the child in the boat cried for its mother

& a man came and took my child and said he would bounce her for me
& I said yes please help my child go to sleep
& my eyes burned
& I couldn't find her
& I slept

IV

FEED

Wind whips the umbrella on the porch like a ship's sail
    I watch it twist and lean over the counter eating numb-eyed

        The baby rolls in the monitor's blue fuzz
  and I calculate how long until he needs to eat again

          I've been going for months   If I stop, I will be ordinary
      All I want to do is feed myself bread and milk

      I cut the baby out of the poem
    I put the baby back in

  The geese are migrating somewhere
One lags behind   veering

     unsatisfied by its pocket in the V
       the group's squawking mind to move

         maybe hating those beating bodies ahead
  I need the baby to take a nap   I need the baby to not need me

    I never meant to be so needed
               I dream about drifting   alone
  I can't quiet my ambition
  It bats at my knees and I toss it scraps

     hoping it will reward me for wrenching off each finger
each thick arm   my teeming head

dropping them   one by one   into the black well of its jaws

TO BE A WOMAN

means you aren't really supposed to trust any men   When your
husband leaves the car to buy some water and the Lyft driver hits
the pedal you yell *Not yet! Go back!* He says *I'm just turning around,
Ma'am! Ma'am, please!* You feel like an ass But you were thinking of
the Swiss woman gang-raped in the woods   of the woman on the
bus raped by seven men and a metal rod   of the girl in your math
class   of the five-year-old   alone   for two days in an apartment
below her parents At the gym, you watch a mango juice commercial
Two women with movie-star hair jockey to pour mango juice down
one man's throat   Crouched barely clothed in a green glade skin
glistening beyond delighted.

LIGHTNESS

The feeling of being almost
free   like sitting at a metal desk
a few minutes before summer:

the last feeding of the day
her going quiet   letting go my nipple
so tired but weightless

now I carry only my own body
the husk of the me that was

MY OWN

Can you fix my crown?
        He's Jack I'm Jill

We rolled down the hill

        it broke it all breaks down

A woman drives by alone windows rolled
        bobbing her bright head

A riptide has pulled

        through my skin all day

How do I get out? If I can't get out
        —don't think about that

Keep floating till it thins
        in cold open sea

My meditation app says

        there is always blue sky

even when you can't see it

        We watch a worm roll out

of a rotten tree trunk
body of muscle made

        to tunnel, to escape

Can you fix my crown, Mama?
    Please?

He pretends to pick up a sapphire

        offers it to me

I want to fix his crown
        But I'm trying to fix my own

UP THE ROAD, WOMEN IN DARK DRESSES

pull corn in tall fields like the ones she grew up tending,
and my grandmother waves knotted fingers at my son.

She dangles them like ribboned wands.
His eyes follow for a few seconds, lose interest.

I nurse him in her dark living room — ancestors
with my flecked eyes watching. 1957, my grandmother,

age twenty-two, married in a sensible skirt suit and hat,
red lips flat, not quite a smile.

My husband talks to her on the other side of the wall,
her motorized bed grinding up and down. I want

to do something beautiful for her, sincere as the flower
of my son's mouth slightly open as he sleeps on my breast

something like the way he reaches for my mouth while he eats,
needs to touch my lips, to know I am there and breathing, too.

She is dying and I don't know what to do.
I press a brown velvet pillow to my face to remember,

can't describe the smell seconds after. She is dying and I want
my son to make her smile. But he is serious, grunting and batting

at her purple fleece robe. She helps him clutch
the robe's thick belt. It tightens around my throat.

Everything she might say is locked in her shy neck.
I do not ask the questions I meant to ask. She waves goodbye.

The rented mattress sighs when I stand to go.
The corn along the road bows its many necks goodbye.

DEAR CHARLOTTE

January

Sometimes silence contains
its own dizzying music

AUBADE WITH TEETHER

                                Keys water phone teether

                                         Keys water phone jacket

Sleep fogs the window   pats the car seat

                                    Keys water phone teether

                         Click the baby's seat belt   Click the baby's seat belt

                                             Keys water phone teether

Sleep reaches for you   it would be so nice to—

                                           Snacks water teether—

                  1 mile   1 mile   then left

                                      Water   snacks jackets

Sleep whispers your name   that sly rasp in his voice

                                       Snacks   jackets—

                Exit 65A   Sharp right—

                  Exit 65A   Exit 65   A

Sleep's grip loosens your back

                Kids watching their show   Kids happy

Eyes open   focus   focus—

Sleep licks your ear

                              (left turn) —

                                   (left —)

                                   (left

ISLE OF IONA

Islands beyond islands, so many we can't remember
their names. We trudge to the hilltop hoping
we're close to the sea, and find another hill

swathed in grass prickly as coral.
Out so far nobody would find
us for days, they wouldn't even know

to look. My feet crunch through bushes
and sea holly and he tells me he doesn't believe
his brother is in heaven

he doesn't believe there is a heaven
what we do here now is the point, he says
his back cutting a line against the sea.

He admits he doesn't know, that I
could be a flower eventually, or
a seal. But either way, my body will

be folded into the crumbled soil,
like his brother, how at first everyone
will remember us, and tell our stories

in bars and living rooms, then they
will die, too. We will harden then soften
on a hill like this.

I don't know if I can have children.
If I do, I don't know if they will be healthy,
if they will outlive us.

I want another chance at light.
Why do I need him to admit
there will be more for us?

DRUM

We wait while the car cools
from a day's worth
of beating sun

My daughter stands, bare feet
balancing
on my thighs

We drum the steering wheel
make a clumsy music together

WAKE

My daughter paints grey
moons under my eyes all day.
I nearly tip her out

of the stroller. Her jaw
quivers. I want so many things.
What did my mother want?

I study her hands.
Her left pointer finger
curves in like a leaf.

My daughter sleeps in my
arms, light as a needle.
Her eyes, tiny almonds.

What did my mother regret?
Guilt, a tight ring I can't take off.
At the zoo, the ostrich fixes

its lightbulb eyes on me.
My daughter kicks her legs
into the day's weak light.

Her new eyes follow
leaf shadows in the wind.
Ostriches can't fly.

If attacked, they kick
their knock-kneed legs to survive.
My widowed neighbor, Billie,

stares at my daughter, says,
*To wake up and know someone
like that is waiting for you.*

GIRL IN THE STREET

It's the way water

eats rock

     hey baby why don't you smile?

how it slips inside

a hairline crack

     hey mama suck my dick

splits it wide

from within

     girl can you handle 13 inches?

I want to

wear the jackal's

teeth in the street

its high gaze

but it's just me

a woman walking

in my clogs

and glasses

My daughter just learned to walk

girl where you going?

still unsteady on her feet

baby you got a boyfriend?

she barrels into the street   head first

nice ass girl

shrieking with glee

bitch why don't you smile?

I'm almost 40

girl don't you want some of this?

I should be able to talk back by now

right?

Words break bedrock—

I remember mine—

      fierce slab layered

      with love and yes

     bitch come on back

their voices became

hands   became

dogs became

knives

DEAR CHARLOTTE

May

Things happen and I don't know who to tell.

My brother-in-law, they found him dead in his car
He was driving through the night to see his girlfriend
He fell asleep

The way I hold my son
no hands   my arms as railings
I can read a little

while he shifts his body
near enough that he won't fall
but not so close he's contained

the deer that found his shirt left saliva
and holes where she chewed
and sucked out the salt

the saguaro cactus only blooms at night
bats flock in the dark
to drink

Magnolia blossoms flying off the car
in front of me — they make a pink curtain
I drive through

the guy who collects the grocery carts
hops up and rides each one a little way
before they click into each other

my son leans his face into the machine
that makes bird noises
falls into it   his mouth opening

THE LOST BREAD

They came to Toronto to commune with the dead, or so I heard through the thin wall between us for three mornings, when they shuffled downstairs early to eat breakfast outside our room. They talked and laughed at the man's bass recalling his adventures in Italy, in Fiji, with a healer out west — were silent when he said he hears their voices often (the dead). I tried to sleep, but couldn't drown out his voice calling French toast the *lost bread*. They laughed, so he repeated — *the lost bread*. I never saw their faces. I slept and woke to their voices, a child under the table at a dinner party, staring at feet and making up stories about people's lives from their shoes, the size of their calves. I walked Toronto all day every day, ate Persian food, visited parks and museums, but I kept wondering why the living aren't enough, what the dead have to tell.

YOU TOO

after Agnar Artuvertin

And you too shall sleep through the dark
you who rise to the baby's wail

And you too shall ride a white horse
you whose skin still aches from birth

And you too shall write a whole poem
you who drops sounds here and there

And you too shall be asked back in
you whose door the baby blew shut

NECESSARY CITY

I'm walking in hard rain in East Liberty
        no umbrella   keeping direction by
the Cathedral rising

over the roofs of this city I swore
        I'd never live in.   Nico and Kai shop
in Giant Eagle. I know

he's taking good care of him   probably
        making him laugh   feeding him
cheerios. I could leave   get in my car

and drive away to the big world before
        anyone would realize.
Yesterday I was daydreaming   panicked

and turned too soon   missed
        the Armstrong tunnel and drove up
Mt Washington trying to get to the South Side.

I could see that busy strip bending behind me
        in the mirror   but I was heading high
and away, above the three rivers—

Allegheny and Monongahela rushing
        into the Ohio—a shining
blue body   arms up in surrender

the hills bright with sunset   the fountain
        at the Point plunging
back into concrete, a few people watching

growing smaller and smaller.
　　　　I live in a city I sometimes hate.
I have no job to write on the doctor's forms.

When my child cries　I often freeze.
　　　　I walk toward my family　the smell
of heavy rain in my hair, wanting

a way through—but I chose these people
　　　　who put up with my skittishness.
I want to run toward this city of my life

like the heroine at the end of the film once
　　　　she's learned what really matters.
But I just walk a little faster

counting the lights in old warehouses along
　　　　Centre Avenue bright squares cutting
the grey Pittsburgh air.

IMITATION GAME

He's in charge
He grins, walks backward

I walk backward away from him
He frowns, says *No mama,*
Go backward toward me

I'M TRYING TO WRITE A JOYFUL POEM

after reading Ross Gay's new book,
which makes me feel light
and giddy, like maybe
a world in which figs fall
from a city sky is possible,
but my poem becomes
about the collapse of long
love, how even the brightest
glint in the eye
becomes shadow eventually.
My son dances across
the room in a red
cowboy hat, he asks me
to chase him,
but the girl in the documentary
I watch lives in a landfill
outside Moscow —
she drinks water from
dirty milk jugs and —
why does joy always slide
into darkness?
My son laughs, his eight teeth
new and white, shining in the sun
while I tickle his belly.
Joy must be at least
as complicated as sorrow,
which is one reason
I hate those posed pictures
people take before
weddings, before babies,
hands clasped over the woman's
belly — cupping warm skin

thinking they know
what's inside.

Maybe joy is an animal that scurries
when you get close,
or maybe it's my son
pointing out the moon
saying *Look! Up there!*
which makes me think
how he almost wasn't
so many times.
And doesn't the girl in Moscow,
Yula is her name,
have joys, too?
And this cramped coffee shop
hums with people telling
other people across a stretch
of table what it feels like
to live on this planet right now,
to have a mouth,
to form words — I'm saying,
How are you feeling?
She's saying, *It was just so funny,*
so damn funny
and the woman next to me
she laughs, she sighs,
she holds her belly.

Maybe joy is the real mystery.
Maybe I've been wrong
for decades, only looking
under the rock, pointing out
the shades of dark.
Last night I lay across
from my love and

said *I love you,*
something I usually say
while opening the fridge,
while leaving the house,
my back turned,
I said *I love you*
staring right into
his open eyes —
what made me look
is that I remembered
he will die. Maybe joy
is a hand reaching out
in a fierce wind,
one so very hard
to open your fingers in,
or your eyes.

NOTES & ACKNOWLEDGMENTS

I'm grateful to the editors of the following journals for giving these poems a home, some in different form:

Tupelo Quarterly: "Needlework"
The Adroit Journal: "So Easy"
Poet Lore: "To the Question, 'What Happened?'"
Crab Orchard Review: "Up the Road, Women in Dark Dresses"
New Ohio Review: "I'm trying to write a joyful poem"
Muzzle Magazine: "Feed," "& then she wailed & screamed & coughed on her own drool"
Glass: A Journal of Poetry: "Girl in the Street"
Raleigh Review: "Lightning Flowers"
Cimarron Review: "The Lost Bread"
Peauxdunque Review: "Elliptical Advice," "Window"
Gulf Stream: "Still Life with Ex-Husband Lingering"
Radar Poetry: "Wake"
Connotation Press: "Aubade with Teether," "Lightness," "The Ant's Small Face," "Woman as Column, Fitzwilliam Museum"
Public Pool: "Landscape with Dream, Deer"
DIALOGIST: "Anatomy of Distance"
Rogue Agent Journal: "The Falls"
The Woven Tale Literary and Arts Magazine: "Thunderstart," "Isle of Iona"
Southword Journal: "As Much As a Letter"
Two Horatio #2: "Maybe"
Bridge Eight Literary Magazine: "Wednesday Morning and I am Being Opened"
Pittsburgh City Paper: "To Be a Woman"
Voices from the Attic Anthology, Carlow University: "The Dress-

Preserver," "Blade," "Still Life with Possible Life," "Drowning the Cracks"

Some of the poems in this book appear in *FEED*, winner of the 2018 Keystone Chapbook Prize from Seven Kitchens Press, selected by Steve Bellin-Oka.

The book's epigraph is from "The Quiet House," from Charlotte Mew's *Collected Poems and Selected Prose*, edited by Val Warner, Carcanet Books, 1997.

The italicized line in the final stanza of "Dear Charlotte Mew, July" is from Mew's poem, "A Quoi Bon Dire."

The title "Lightning Flowers" is another name for Lichtenberg figures—fernlike patterns that often appear on the skin of lightning strike victims.

"Dear Charlotte (November)" uses a few lines from Mew's poems, including "Rooms," "Fame," and "The Quiet House."

"Kindreds" is for Shannon Young.

"Up the Road, Women in Dark Dresses" is for Dorothy Koss Mohn.

"Wake" is for Billie Lozano.

"Girl in the Street" is for all the women and girls just trying to get somewhere.

"I'm trying to write a joyful poem" is for Nico Slate.

Thank you to David Bowen and everyone at New American Press for believing in this book and for bringing it into the world. Thank you to Sara Gelston for picking this manuscript out of the pile. Thank you to Charli Barnes for your stunning cover art and design work.

Thank you to my English teachers, who saw something in me and encouraged me to keep reading and writing: Mrs. Shevchik, Mrs. Purviance, Dr. Brozick, Mr. Baier.

Thank you to my Bennington teachers: April Bernard, Major Jackson, Mark Wunderlich, and Ed Ochester, for your example, for your wise teaching and inspiration.

Thank you to my Pittsburgh poetry teachers: especially Jan Beatty, whose teaching and mentorship gave me the courage to risk it, and to Nancy Krygowski and Stacey Waite, for pushing my poems to new places.

Thank you to all my fellow Madwomen in the Attic writers and teachers, for giving so much to these poems and to me over the last nine years, and for your devotion to poetry and community— especially Liane Ellison Norman, CJ Coleman (we miss you fiercely), Barbara Dahlberg, Alexandra Kemrer, Amanda Brant, Daniela Buccilli, Kayla Sargeson, Celeste Gainey, Jane McCafferty, Joy Katz, M.A. Sinnhuber, Molly Bain, Victoria Dym, Maritza Mosquera, Bonita Lee Penn, Valerie Bacharach, Joan Bauer, Sheila Carter-Jones, Arlene Weiner, Anne Rashid, Sarah Williams-Devereaux.

Thank you to Jan Beatty, Barbara Dahlberg, Wendy Scott, Teresa Narey, and Katie Filicky for your smart comments on the earliest draft of the manuscript that became this book.

Thank you to my Bennington friends for the inspiration of your own work, for your unwavering friendship, and for dancing. You are gold.

Thank you to the Josephine Street Poets: Tess Barry, Rachel Mennies, Lisa Alexander, Michelle Stoner, Jennifer Jackson Berry,

Bernadette Ulsamer—for your championing early drafts of many of these poems, and for the pure love of poetry you bring to our time around Tess's table.

Thank you to Cassie Pruyn, Jennifer Stewart Miller, Joanne Proulx, and Denton Loving, The Dream Team: brilliant writers, fierce editors, the truest friends, for always picking me up, for your help in making each one of these poems far better than it otherwise would have been. For helping me keep going.

Thank you to Ron Mohring and Steve Bellin-Oka for choosing my chapbook, *FEED*, which is one of the beating hearts of this book.

Thank you to Jill and Adlai Yeomans, and Anna Claire Weber at White Whale Bookstore in Bloomfield, for your magical bookstore, for making thousands of readings happen, and for tirelessly championing writers and small presses.

Thank you to my students and colleagues at Chatham, CMU, Winchester Thurston, and around Pittsburgh—for teaching me, for keeping me grounded in why we write.

Thank you to the talented teachers at the Cyert Center for Early Education at CMU, the Ellis School, and the Jewish Community Center of PGH, for caring for and teaching my children while I worked on many of these poems.

Thank you to my late grandmother, Dorothy Koss Mohn, and my aunt, Connie Mohn, for seeing me as a writer from the earliest point.

Thank you to my dear friends, Shannon Young, Hana Lewis, Heidi Hayes Paré, Jennifer Beale, Susie Meister, Nancy Boldt McLaren, Katie Luczak, and Mary Kuhn: for keeping me honest, for making me laugh, and for loving me as I am for all these years.

Thank you to my parents, Ann and Kim Mohn, my brother, Matt Mohn and sister-in law, Lauren Mohn, my sister, Casey Calland and brother-in-law, Mat Calland, my mother-in-law, Karena Slate, and my whole big, loud extended family: for loving me no matter what, for giving me a strong foundation I can always lean on.

Thank you to my children, Kai and Lucia, who have inspired me to write many of these poems, who constantly pull me to the present.

And, thank you to Nico for believing in me when I do not believe in myself, for pushing me to do what scares me, for your steadfast support of my writing and my dreams. Thank you for sharing this life with me.

EMILY MOHN-SLATE is the author of *FEED*, which won the 2018 Keystone Chapbook Prize (Seven Kitchens Press). Her poems and essays have appeared or are forthcoming in *AGNI*, *New Ohio Review*, *The Adroit Journal*, *Tupelo Quarterly*, *Poet Lore*, and elsewhere. She's a graduate of the Bennington Writing Seminars (MFA), Boston University (MA), and Colgate University (BA). She lives in Pittsburgh, PA, where she teaches high school English at Winchester Thurston School, and teaches poetry workshops in Carlow University's Madwomen in the Attic writing program. *THE FALLS* is her debut poetry collection.